JEANNE HOUSTON

ADHD in the Workplace: A Guide to Living Presently

A Guide to Living Presently

Copyright © 2023 by Jeanne Houston

All rights reserved. No part of this publication may be reproduced, stored or transmitted in any form or by any means, electronic, mechanical, photocopying, recording, scanning, or otherwise without written permission from the publisher. It is illegal to copy this book, post it to a website, or distribute it by any other means without permission.

First edition

This book was professionally typeset on Reedsy. Find out more at reedsy.com

Contents

I Understanding ADHD

1 Introduction	3
2 What is ADHD?	6
3 ADHD in Women	10

II Navigating the Workspace

4 Job Selection	15
5 The Interview Process	19
6 Workplace Accommodations	22

III Skill Building

7 Time Management	27
8 How to stay organized	30
9 Communication	33

IV Self-Advocacy and Networking

10 Advocating for Yourself	39
11 Networking Strategies	43

V Mental and Emotional Well-being

12 Stress Management   49
13 Building Self-Esteem   52

VI Career Advancement

14 Climbing the Corporate Ladder   57
15 Entrepreneurship and ADHD   60

VII Special Circumstances

16 Remote Work and ADHD   65
17 Navigating Career Transitions   68

VIII Future Outlook

18 ADHD and the Evolving Workplace   73
19 Lifelong Learning and Development 76

IX Conclusion

20 Your ADHD, Your Success   83

I

Understanding ADHD

1

Introduction

Welcome to "ADHD in the Workplace: A Guide to Living Presently." If you've picked up this book, chances are you're a woman navigating the professional world with Attention-Deficit/Hyperactivity Disorder (ADHD), or you know someone who is. The journey through the workplace can be a challenging one, filled with obstacles that seem insurmountable. However, it's important to remember that you're not alone, and your unique neurodiversity can also be a source of incredible strength.

Purpose of the Book

The primary aim of this book is to serve as a comprehensive guide for women with ADHD who are striving for success in their professional lives. Whether you're entering the job market for the first time, seeking to advance in your current position, or contemplating a career change, this book is designed to be your go-to resource. It covers a wide range of topics, from understanding the nuances of ADHD and how it manifests in women, to practical advice on job selection, self-advocacy, and skill-building.

What You Can Expect to Gain

By the end of this book, you will have a deeper understanding of:

1. **What ADHD is and How it Affects Women Differently**: The first part of the book demystifies ADHD, dispelling common myths and providing insights into how ADHD symptoms can manifest differently in women compared to men.
2. **Navigating the Professional Landscape:** Learn how to select a job that aligns with your ADHD traits, ace interviews, and understand your legal rights when it comes to workplace accommodations.
3. **Skill Building**: Master essential skills like time management, organization, and effective communication, tailored to the unique challenges that women with ADHD face.
4. **Self-Advocacy and Networking**: Discover how to advocate for yourself in the workplace, build a supportive network, and employ effective networking strategies that can advance your career.
5. **Mental and Emotional Well-being**: Gain tools for managing stress and building self-esteem, crucial for long-term career success and personal development.
6. **Career Advancement**: Get actionable advice on climbing the corporate ladder, preparing for leadership roles, and even venturing into entrepreneurship.
7. **Special Circumstances**: Whether you're working remotely, transitioning careers, or re-entering the workforce, this book offers specialized advice for those unique situations.
8. **Future Outlook**: Understand how the workplace is evolving to become more inclusive and how you can prepare for these changes.

In addition to these core areas, the book includes case studies, real-life

INTRODUCTION

examples, and practical exercises to help you apply what you've learned.

So, are you ready to turn your ADHD into an asset and achieve unprecedented success in your professional life? Let's embark on this journey together.

Thank you for choosing "ADHD in the Workplace: A Woman's Guide to Career Success" as your companion on this exciting journey. Let's get started!

2

What is ADHD?

Welcome to the first chapter of "ADHD in the Workplace: A Woman's Guide to Career Success." Before we delve into the intricacies of navigating the professional world with ADHD, it's crucial to have a solid understanding of what ADHD actually is. This chapter aims to provide you with a comprehensive overview of ADHD, its symptoms, and common misconceptions that often cloud the public's understanding of this neurodevelopmental disorder.

Definition of ADHD

Attention-Deficit/Hyperactivity Disorder (ADHD) is a neurodevelopmental disorder that affects both children and adults, although it often goes undiagnosed until later in life. It is characterized by persistent patterns of inattention, hyperactivity, and impulsivity that interfere with daily functioning or development.

ADHD is generally divided into three subtypes:

1. **Predominantly Inattentive Presentation**: Difficulties with attention, such as forgetfulness, distractibility, and difficulty

sustaining attention in tasks.
2. **Predominantly Hyperactive-Impulsive Presentation**: Symptoms mainly involve hyperactivity, such as fidgeting, and impulsivity, like interrupting others or making hasty decisions without considering the consequences.
3. **Combined Presentation**: This subtype includes symptoms of both inattention and hyperactivity-impulsivity.

It's important to note that ADHD is a medical diagnosis made by healthcare professionals based on specific criteria outlined in the Diagnostic and Statistical Manual of Mental Disorders (DSM-5).

Symptoms

The symptoms of ADHD can vary widely among individuals and may change over time. However, some of the most common symptoms include:

- **Inattention**: Difficulty sustaining attention, frequent careless mistakes, forgetfulness, losing things necessary for tasks.
- **Hyperactivity**: Excessive fidgeting, inability to stay seated in situations where it's expected, running or climbing in inappropriate situations.
- **Impulsivity**: Difficulty waiting one's turn, blurting out answers, and interrupting others.

For women, ADHD symptoms may manifest differently and can often be more subtle, making them harder to diagnose. For example, hyperactivity in women might not be as overt and could manifest as excessive talking or inner restlessness. Inattention might appear as disorganization or forgetfulness.

Common Misconceptions

Unfortunately, ADHD is often misunderstood, leading to a variety of misconceptions. Some of the most common myths include:

1. **ADHD is Just for Kids**: While ADHD is often diagnosed in childhood, many adults continue to experience symptoms and may even get diagnosed later in life.
2. **People with ADHD are Just Lazy**: The challenges faced by individuals with ADHD are neurological, not a matter of willpower. Labeling them as lazy is both inaccurate and harmful.
3. **ADHD is Overdiagnosed**: While awareness of ADHD has increased, that doesn't mean it's overdiagnosed. Many people, especially women, go undiagnosed and untreated.
4. **Medication is the Only Treatment**: While medication can be effective, it's often most beneficial as part of a multi-faceted treatment approach that can include behavioral therapy, lifestyle changes, and accommodations.
5. **ADHD is a "Gift"**: While many people with ADHD have unique strengths, it's important to recognize that ADHD is a medical condition that can cause significant challenges.
6. **Women Don't Get ADHD**: This is a particularly damaging misconception. Women can and do have ADHD; however, their symptoms may manifest differently, making diagnosis more challenging.

Understanding ADHD is the first step in managing it effectively, especially in the workplace. As we move through this book, we'll explore how you can leverage your understanding of ADHD to your advantage in a professional setting, turning perceived weaknesses into strengths.

Thank you for taking the time to understand the basics of ADHD. In the next chapter, we will delve deeper into how ADHD affects women specifically, both in daily life and in the workplace.

3

ADHD in Women

Welcome to the this chapter of "ADHD in the Workplace: A Woman's Guide to Career Success." Now that we have a foundational understanding of what ADHD is, it's time to explore how this neurodevelopmental disorder manifests differently in women. This chapter will also delve into the impact of societal expectations on women with ADHD, which can add an extra layer of complexity to both diagnosis and management.

How ADHD Manifests Differently in Women

While the core symptoms of ADHD—namely inattention, hyperactivity, and impulsivity—are consistent across genders, the way these symptoms manifest and are perceived can differ significantly between men and women. Here are some key differences:

1. **Subtler Symptoms**: Women often exhibit less overt symptoms than men. For example, hyperactivity in women may not involve running around but could manifest as talkativeness, emotional turbulence, or an inner feeling of restlessness.
2. **Internalization**: Women are more likely to internalize their

symptoms, leading to issues like low self-esteem, anxiety, and depression. This can sometimes result in a misdiagnosis, where the underlying ADHD is overlooked.
3. **Executive Function Challenges**: While men with ADHD also struggle with executive functions like planning and organization, women often find these issues particularly debilitating, especially when juggling multiple roles at home and at work.
4. **Emotional Dysregulation**: Though not an official criterion for ADHD diagnosis, emotional dysregulation—extreme emotional sensitivity and strong emotional reactions—can be a significant issue for women with ADHD.
5. **Late Diagnosis**: Women are often diagnosed later in life compared to men, usually during late adolescence or even adulthood. This is often because their symptoms are less disruptive and may not have been flagged during childhood.
6. **Coexisting Conditions**: Women with ADHD are more likely to have coexisting conditions like eating disorders, anxiety, and depression, which can complicate the diagnostic process.

The Impact of Societal Expectations

Societal norms and expectations can exacerbate the challenges faced by women with ADHD. Here are some ways in which societal expectations impact women:

1. **The "Perfect Woman" Myth**: Society often expects women to be organized, nurturing, and adept at multitasking. For women with ADHD, these expectations can be overwhelming and lead to feelings of inadequacy.
2. **Stigma and Misunderstanding**: There's a societal misconception that ADHD is a "boy's disorder," which can make it harder for

women to seek help or even realize that they might have ADHD.
3. **Workplace Challenges**: In professional settings, women are often judged more harshly for disorganization or perceived lack of focus, which can hinder career progression.
4. **Parenting Pressures**: Mothers with ADHD may find the demands of parenting especially challenging, yet they often face societal scrutiny if they struggle with organization or emotional regulation.
5. **Intersectionality**: Women of color, LGBTQ+ women, and women from various cultural backgrounds may face additional layers of complexity and bias when it comes to ADHD diagnosis and treatment.

Understanding how ADHD manifests differently in women and acknowledging the impact of societal expectations are crucial steps in effectively managing ADHD symptoms. This knowledge not only aids in accurate diagnosis but also helps in tailoring treatment plans that address the unique challenges faced by women with ADHD.

In the next chapter, we will discuss the journey to getting an ADHD diagnosis, which can be a pivotal moment in the life of a woman with ADHD. We'll explore the steps involved, the professionals you might consult, and what to expect during the diagnostic process.

Thank you for joining us in this important discussion. Your journey to understanding and managing ADHD in a way that aligns with your professional goals is well underway.

II

Navigating the Workspace

4

Job Selection

One of the most pivotal decisions in life is choosing a career path. For women with ADHD, this decision can be both challenging and exciting. In this chapter, we'll delve into the intricacies of job selection, focusing on how to align your unique ADHD traits with a fulfilling career. We'll also explore the pros and cons of various job types, providing you with a comprehensive guide to making an informed decision.

Choosing a Career that Suits Your ADHD Traits

Every individual with ADHD is unique, and while there are common symptoms, the way they manifest and influence one's strengths and challenges can vary. Here's a guide to aligning your ADHD traits with a career:

1. **Recognize Your Strengths**: Many with ADHD are creative, think outside the box, and can hyper-focus on tasks they're passionate about. Careers in arts, design, or entrepreneurial ventures might be suitable.
2. **Understand Your Challenges**: If you struggle with organization,

a job that requires meticulous administrative skills might not be ideal. Instead, roles that allow for big-picture thinking could be more fitting.
3. **Seek Dynamic Environments**: Many with ADHD thrive in dynamic, ever-changing environments. Jobs in event planning, journalism, or emergency services might be appealing.
4. **Consider Flexibility**: The traditional 9-to-5 might not suit everyone with ADHD. Careers that offer flexible hours or remote working can be beneficial.
5. **Feedback and Recognition**: If you thrive on immediate feedback, careers in sales, marketing, or customer service, where results are instantly measurable, might be suitable.

Pros and Cons of Various Job Types

Let's delve into some common job types, examining their potential advantages and disadvantages for women with ADHD:

1. **Creative Roles (e.g., Designer, Writer, Artist)**

- **Pros**: Allows for self-expression, often flexible hours, can work on multiple projects.
- **Cons**: Deadlines can be stressful, may require self-promotion, income might be inconsistent.

1. **Administrative Roles (e.g., Office Manager, Executive Assistant)**

- **Pros**: Structured environment, clear tasks, regular working hours.
- **Cons**: Requires high organization, repetitive tasks might feel monotonous, potential for distractions in busy environments.

1. **Entrepreneurial Ventures**

- **Pros**: Complete autonomy, flexibility, potential for high rewards, can choose projects that align with passions.
- **Cons**: Financial instability, requires self-discipline, multitasking across various business aspects.

1. **Healthcare and Emergency Services (e.g., Nurse, Paramedic)**

- **Pros**: Dynamic environment, immediate feedback, opportunity to make a difference.
- **Cons**: Long hours, high stress, requires quick decision-making.

1. **Teaching and Education**

- **Pros**: Opportunity to shape minds, structured academic year, diverse tasks.
- **Cons**: Requires planning and organization, potential for classroom disruptions, administrative tasks.

1. **Sales and Marketing**

- **Pros**: Immediate feedback, potential for high rewards, dynamic environment.
- **Cons**: Can be target-driven, requires networking, potential for inconsistent income.

When choosing a career, it's essential to remember that no job is perfect. Every role will have its challenges and rewards. The key is to find a career that aligns closely with your strengths, passions, and lifestyle preferences while being mindful of potential challenges. It's also worth noting that career paths are rarely linear. As you grow and evolve, so too might your career aspirations.

In the next chapter, we'll explore the interview process, providing you with strategies and insights to present your ADHD as a strength and secure your desired role.

Thank you for joining us on this journey of job selection. With the right knowledge and self-awareness, you're well on your way to finding a career that not only accommodates but celebrates your unique ADHD traits.

5

The Interview Process

Having explored the nuances of job selection, it's time to focus on the next critical step: the interview process. Interviews can be nerve-wracking for anyone, but for women with ADHD, they present a unique set of challenges and opportunities. In this chapter, we'll discuss how to prepare for interviews effectively and how to present your ADHD as a strength rather than a hindrance.

Preparing for Interviews

Preparation is key to succeeding in job interviews. Here are some tailored tips to help you prepare:

1. **Research the Company**: Understanding the company's culture, mission, and the role you're applying for can help you tailor your responses and show that you're genuinely interested.
2. **Practice Common Questions**: While you can't predict every question, practicing answers to common interview questions can help you feel more confident.
3. **Organize Your Thoughts**: Women with ADHD often have a

wealth of ideas but may struggle with organizing them. Consider creating a 'cheat sheet' of key points you want to cover during the interview.
4. **Mock Interviews**: Conducting mock interviews with a friend or family member can help you get comfortable with the interview format.
5. **Plan Your Journey**: Knowing the interview location, how to get there, and how long the journey will take can reduce stress on the day.
6. **Prepare Your Outfit**: Choose an outfit that is appropriate for the job and makes you feel confident. Prepare it the night before to avoid last-minute stress.
7. **Mindfulness Techniques**: If you're feeling anxious, techniques such as deep breathing or visualization can help calm your nerves before the interview.

How to Present Your ADHD as a Strength

Discussing ADHD in a job interview is a personal choice and depends on various factors, including the job requirements and the company culture. If you choose to disclose your ADHD, here's how to present it as a strength:

1. **Focus on Skills, Not Labels**: Instead of saying, "I have ADHD," you could say, "I excel in dynamic environments and am great at thinking outside the box."
2. **Highlight Adaptability**: Many people with ADHD are highly adaptable, a skill that is valuable in today's rapidly changing workplace.
3. **Discuss Your Unique Perspective**: ADHD often comes with a unique way of viewing problems, which can lead to innovative

solutions.
4. **Talk About Hyperfocus**: When interested in a task, many with ADHD can hyperfocus, diving deep into projects and achieving excellent results.
5. **Show Self-Awareness**: If the role requires skills that can be challenging with ADHD, like meticulous organization, discuss the strategies you've developed to manage these challenges effectively.
6. **Use Past Experiences**: Provide examples from your previous roles where your ADHD traits have been an asset. This could be a project you excelled in or a problem you solved creatively.
7. **Be Honest but Positive**: If directly asked about weaknesses or challenges, be honest but always follow up with how you're actively managing these aspects and turning them into strengths.

The interview process is not just about the employer finding the right candidate; it's also about you finding a job and environment where you can thrive. By adequately preparing and strategically presenting your ADHD traits, you can increase your chances of achieving just that.

In the next chapter, we will delve into the topic of workplace accommodations, exploring your legal rights and how to request accommodations that can set you up for success.

Thank you for joining us in this chapter. With the right preparation and mindset, you're well-equipped to shine in your interviews and take a significant step toward a fulfilling career.

6

Workplace Accommodations

Now that we've covered the interview process, it's time to focus on what happens after you land the job. One of the most crucial aspects of workplace success for women with ADHD is understanding and utilizing workplace accommodations. In this chapter, we'll explore your legal rights concerning workplace accommodations, how to request them, and examples of effective accommodations that can make a significant difference in your professional life.

Legal Rights

In the United States, the Americans with Disabilities Act (ADA) protects employees with disabilities, including ADHD, from discrimination in the workplace. This law also requires employers to provide "reasonable accommodations" to qualified applicants or employees with a disability unless it would cause significant difficulty or expense for the employer ("undue hardship").

1. **Disclosure**: Legally, you are not required to disclose your ADHD to your employer unless you are seeking accommodations. The

decision to disclose is personal and should be carefully considered.
2. **Documentation**: If you decide to request accommodations, you may need to provide documentation of your ADHD diagnosis. This usually involves a letter from a healthcare provider outlining the accommodations that would be beneficial for you.
3. **Confidentiality**: Employers are required to keep all medical information confidential and can only share it with staff who need to know to provide the accommodation.

How to Request Accommodations

1. **Timing**: You can request accommodations at any time during the employment process, although it's often easier after a job offer has been extended.
2. **Written Request**: While verbal requests are acceptable, it's advisable to make your request in writing for documentation purposes. Outline the specific challenges you face and the accommodations that would help.
3. **Consult with HR**: Your Human Resources department is usually the first point of contact for accommodation requests. They can guide you through the process and let you know what documentation is needed.
4. **Interactive Process**: The ADA encourages an "interactive process," a dialogue between you and your employer to determine effective accommodations.
5. **Review and Adjust**: Accommodations may need to be reviewed and adjusted over time. Keep an open line of communication with your employer to ensure that the accommodations are meeting your needs.

Examples of Effective Accommodations

1. **Flexible Scheduling**: Adjusting your work hours to align with your most productive times of the day.
2. **Remote Work Options**: The ability to work from home on certain days can minimize distractions and improve focus.
3. **Breaks and Quiet Spaces**: Scheduled short breaks or access to a quiet space can help manage symptoms of hyperactivity and improve concentration.
4. **Task Management Tools**: Utilizing digital tools or apps that can help you manage your tasks and deadlines more effectively.
5. **Written Instructions**: Receiving instructions in written form can help if you struggle with memory or attention.
6. **Regular Feedback**: Scheduled check-ins with your supervisor can provide you with the feedback you may need to stay on track.
7. **Job Restructuring**: Shifting non-essential tasks to other employees to allow you to focus on tasks that align with your strengths.

Understanding your rights and knowing how to request accommodations are vital steps in setting yourself up for success in the workplace. These accommodations are not special privileges but tools that level the playing field, allowing you to showcase your skills and contributions effectively.

In the next chapter, we'll delve into skill-building techniques tailored for women with ADHD, focusing on time management, organization, and effective communication.

Thank you for joining us in this important chapter. Armed with this knowledge, you're well on your way to creating a work environment where you can truly thrive.

III

Skill Building

7

Time Management

Time management is a skill that many people struggle with, but for women with ADHD, it can be a particularly challenging aspect of professional life. However, with the right strategies and tools, you can turn this potential weakness into a strength. In this chapter, we'll explore various techniques for managing your time effectively and introduce some tools and apps that can make the process easier.

Strategies for Managing Time Effectively

1. **Prioritize Tasks**: Not all tasks are created equal. Use a system like the Eisenhower Box to categorize tasks as urgent/important, important/not urgent, urgent/not important, or neither. Focus on the important tasks that align with your goals.
2. **Time Blocking**: Allocate specific blocks of time to different tasks or types of work. This can help you avoid multitasking, which is often less efficient than focusing on one thing at a time.
3. **The Pomodoro Technique**: Work in bursts of intense focus (usually 25 minutes, known as 'Pomodoros') separated by 5-minute breaks. This can help maintain your attention and prevent

burnout.

4. **Set Deadlines**: Even for tasks that don't have external deadlines, set your own. This creates a sense of urgency that can help you stay focused.
5. **Batch Similar Tasks**: Group similar tasks together and tackle them in a single time block. This reduces the mental load of switching between different types of activities.
6. **Eliminate Distractions**: Identify your main distractions and work on eliminating or minimizing them. This could mean turning off social media notifications or creating a dedicated workspace.
7. **Use a Timer**: For tasks you dread, set a timer for a short period (e.g., 10 minutes) and commit to working on the task for that time. Often, starting is the hardest part.
8. **Reflect and Adjust**: At the end of each day or week, reflect on what you've accomplished and what could be improved. Use these insights to adjust your strategies.

Tools and Apps That Can Help

1. **Google Calendar**: Use it for time blocking and setting reminders for important tasks and deadlines.
2. **Todoist**: A task management app that allows you to categorize and prioritize tasks, set deadlines, and even collaborate with others.
3. **Focus@Will**: A music app designed to improve concentration by playing background tracks that are optimized to boost focus.
4. **Forest**: An app that discourages you from using your phone by growing a virtual tree that dies if you exit the app before a set time.
5. **Trello**: A project management tool that uses boards, lists, and cards to organize tasks and projects.
6. **RescueTime**: Tracks how you spend your time on your devices, providing insights into your habits and helping you identify time-

wasters.
7. **Evernote**: A note-taking app that can sync across devices, useful for jotting down ideas, plans, and to-do lists.
8. **Clockify**: A time-tracking app that helps you measure how much time you spend on different tasks, providing data that can help you improve your time management strategies.

Time management is a skill that takes time to develop, especially if you're working against ADHD tendencies like impulsivity and distractibility. However, with the right strategies and tools, it's entirely possible to take control of your time and, by extension, your career.

In the next chapter, we'll explore another crucial skill: organization. We'll provide tips and strategies to help you keep both your workspace and your tasks neatly arranged, boosting your efficiency and reducing stress.

Thank you for joining us in this chapter. With these time management strategies and tools, you're well-equipped to make the most of each day, setting the stage for long-term career success.

8

How to stay organized

If time management is the "when" of productivity, organization is the "where" and "how." For women with ADHD, staying organized can be a significant hurdle, but it's also an essential skill for career success. In this chapter, we'll offer tips for maintaining an organized workspace and provide guidance on managing both paperwork and digital files effectively.

Tips for Staying Organized at Work

1. **Designate a Place for Everything**: Whether it's office supplies, keys, or important documents, make sure everything has a designated place. This reduces the time and stress involved in searching for items.
2. **Use Visual Reminders**: Post-it notes, whiteboards, or visual to-do lists can serve as constant reminders of tasks and deadlines.
3. **Declutter Regularly**: Make it a habit to declutter your workspace at least once a week. Remove unnecessary items and reorganize what's left.
4. **Color-Code**: Use different colors for different types of tasks or

projects. This can be applied to your calendar, folders, or even your email inbox.
5. **Daily Planning**: Spend the first or last 10 minutes of your workday planning the next. Outline the tasks you need to complete and prioritize them.
6. **Use Physical Organizers**: Drawer dividers, desktop organizers, and filing cabinets can help keep your physical workspace tidy.
7. **Limit Multitasking**: While it might seem like you're being more productive, multitasking often leads to errors and disorganization. Focus on one task at a time.
8. **Set Organizational Goals**: Just like you have career goals, set organizational goals. Whether it's maintaining a clean desk for a week or effectively using a new productivity app, celebrate these small victories.

How to Manage Paperwork and Digital Files

1. **Paperwork**

- **Filing System**: Create a filing system with clearly labeled folders for different types of documents, such as contracts, invoices, and project plans.
- **Immediate Action**: As soon as you receive a new piece of paper, decide whether to file it, act on it, or discard it. Avoid creating piles of "to be sorted" papers.
- **Scan and Store**: For important documents, consider scanning them and storing digital copies as a backup.

1. **Digital Files**

- **Folder Structure**: Create a logical folder structure on your

computer. Use sub-folders to categorize files further.
- **File Naming**: Use descriptive file names that make it easy to identify the content. Include dates in the file name for version control.
- **Cloud Storage**: Use cloud storage services like Google Drive or Dropbox for important files. This not only serves as a backup but also allows you to access files from anywhere.
- **Regular Clean-Up**: Just like physical clutter, digital clutter can be overwhelming. Set aside time each month to go through your files and delete or archive those you no longer need.

Organization is not a one-time task but an ongoing process. It requires consistent effort, especially for those with ADHD. However, the benefits—increased productivity, reduced stress, and a sense of control over your work environment—are well worth the effort.

In the next chapter, we'll delve into the topic of networking and relationship-building, another crucial aspect of career success for women with ADHD.

Thank you for joining us in this chapter. Armed with these organizational tips and strategies, you're well on your way to creating a more structured and efficient work environment, setting the stage for continued career growth.

9

Communication

Communication is the cornerstone of any successful career, but for women with ADHD, it can present unique challenges. Whether it's maintaining focus during meetings or navigating the complexities of workplace relationships, effective communication is crucial. In this chapter, we'll explore strategies for communicating effectively and tips for managing relationships in the professional setting.

Effective Communication Strategies

1. **Active Listening**: One of the most important aspects of communication is listening. Practice active listening by maintaining eye contact, nodding, and providing verbal cues ("I see," "Go on") to show that you're engaged.
2. **Be Concise**: Women with ADHD sometimes struggle with impulsivity and may speak before thinking. Try to be concise and to the point, avoiding tangential thoughts that may confuse the listener.
3. **Non-Verbal Cues**: Pay attention to your body language. Maintain an open posture, make eye contact, and use gestures to emphasize your points.

4. **Ask for Clarification**: If you're unsure about something, don't hesitate to ask for clarification. It's better to ask questions upfront than to make assumptions that could lead to mistakes.
5. **Follow-Up in Writing**: After important conversations or meetings, it's helpful to send a follow-up email summarizing the key points and next steps. This not only serves as a record but also helps in case you forget details.
6. **Pause Before Responding**: Take a moment to collect your thoughts before responding, especially in emotionally charged situations. This can help you articulate your thoughts more clearly and avoid impulsivity.
7. **Use Visual Aids**: If you're presenting information, consider using visual aids like slides or handouts. This can help keep your audience's attention and also serve as a guide for you.
8. **Practice Empathy**: Try to understand things from the other person's perspective. This can help you tailor your communication in a way that resonates with them.

Navigating Workplace Relationships

1. **Set Boundaries**: Make your needs and limits clear to your colleagues. This is especially important for women with ADHD, who may struggle with time management and distractions.
2. **Be Reliable**: Consistency is key in building trust. If you commit to something, make sure you follow through.
3. **Seek Feedback**: Don't shy away from asking for feedback, both positive and negative. This can provide valuable insights into how you're perceived in the workplace.
4. **Conflict Resolution**: If you find yourself in a conflict, address it directly but diplomatically. Avoid gossiping or discussing the issue with others who are not directly involved.

5. **Network**: Build relationships not just within your immediate team but across the organization. Attend company events, participate in team-building activities, and engage in cross-departmental projects when possible.
6. **Mentorship**: Consider finding a mentor within the organization. This can provide you with valuable career advice and also improve your visibility within the company.
7. **Be Yourself**: Authenticity is important in any relationship. While it's important to maintain a professional demeanor, don't be afraid to let your personality shine through.

Communication is a skill that can always be improved, and for women with ADHD, honing this skill can make a significant difference in career success. From effective listening to managing workplace relationships, each interaction offers an opportunity for growth and improvement.

In the next chapter, we'll discuss career advancement strategies, focusing on how you can leverage your unique skills and navigate the challenges that come with climbing the corporate ladder.

IV

Self-Advocacy and Networking

10

Advocating for Yourself

One of the most empowering skills you can develop in your career is the ability to advocate for yourself. For women with ADHD, this is especially crucial, as you may face unique challenges that require specific accommodations or support. In this chapter, we'll delve into the art of speaking up and asking for what you need, as well as the importance of building a support network.

How to Speak Up and Ask for What You Need

1. **Identify Your Needs**: The first step in advocating for yourself is understanding what you actually need. This could be anything from requesting a quieter workspace to asking for more flexible hours. Take some time to assess what would make your work life more manageable and fulfilling.
2. **Gather Evidence**: Once you've identified your needs, gather evidence to support your request. This could be performance metrics, examples of similar accommodations made for others, or medical documentation in the case of requesting disability accommodations.

3. **Choose the Right Time and Place**: Timing and setting matter. Choose a moment when both you and the person you're speaking to can focus on the conversation, such as during a scheduled one-on-one meeting.
4. **Be Clear and Specific**: When you make your request, be as clear and specific as possible. Vague or ambiguous requests are easier to dismiss.
5. **Use "I" Statements**: Frame the conversation in terms of your own experiences and needs, avoiding blaming or accusing others. For example, say "I find it challenging to focus in a noisy environment" instead of "The office is too loud."
6. **Be Prepared for Questions**: Anticipate questions or objections and prepare your responses in advance. The more prepared you are, the more confident you'll feel.
7. **Follow Up**: After the conversation, send a follow-up email summarizing what was discussed and agreed upon. This creates a written record and shows that you're serious about your request.
8. **Know Your Rights**: Familiarize yourself with any laws or company policies that may support your request, such as the Americans with Disabilities Act (ADA).
9. **Be Persistent but Flexible**: You may not get what you ask for right away, and that's okay. Be prepared to negotiate and offer alternative solutions.

Building a Support Network

1. **Identify Allies**: Look for people within your organization who can be advocates or allies. This could be a supportive manager, a colleague, or even someone in a different department who understands your challenges.
2. **Seek External Support**: Don't limit your support network to

people within your organization. Professional associations, online forums, and social media groups can offer valuable support and advice.
3. **Mentorship and Coaching**: Consider seeking a mentor or coach who has experience navigating the challenges you're facing. Their guidance can be invaluable.
4. **Family and Friends**: Don't underestimate the power of a strong personal support network. Family and friends can offer emotional support and practical advice.
5. **Healthcare Providers**: If you're dealing with ADHD or any other medical condition, a healthcare provider can be an important part of your support network, offering treatment options and documentation to support workplace accommodations.
6. **Build Reciprocal Relationships**: A support network is a two-way street. Look for ways to offer support to others, whether it's through your time, your skills, or your emotional support.
7. **Keep Networking**: Your needs and challenges will evolve over time, and so should your support network. Keep an eye out for new networking opportunities and don't be afraid to reach out for support when you need it.

Advocating for yourself is not about being confrontational or demanding; it's about recognizing your worth and taking steps to achieve the work-life balance and career growth you deserve. Coupled with a strong support network, self-advocacy can be a game-changer in your professional journey.

In the next chapter, we'll explore the topic of career advancement, focusing on how to set achievable goals and work your way up the career ladder, even when faced with the challenges of ADHD.

Thank you for joining us in this comprehensive chapter. With these strategies for self-advocacy and building a support network, you're well-equipped to navigate the complexities of the professional world, ensuring that your unique needs are met and your valuable talents are recognized.

11

Networking Strategies

Networking is often cited as one of the most effective ways to advance your career, yet it can be particularly challenging for women with ADHD. The social nuances, the need for follow-up, and the general hustle of networking events can be overwhelming. However, with the right strategies and tools, you can turn networking from a dreaded task into a powerful asset. In this chapter, we'll explore tips for effective networking and how to leverage social media to your advantage.

Tips for Effective Networking

1. **Set Clear Objectives**: Before attending a networking event or setting up an informational interview, know what you want to achieve. Are you looking for a job, advice, or simply expanding your professional circle?
2. **Prepare Your Elevator Pitch**: Have a concise and compelling description of who you are, what you do, and what you're looking for. This 30-second pitch can make a lasting impression.
3. **Quality Over Quantity**: Networking isn't about collecting as many business cards as possible; it's about forming meaningful

connections. Focus on having in-depth conversations with fewer people rather than spreading yourself thin.
4. **Active Listening**: As discussed in previous chapters, active listening is crucial. Show genuine interest in the other person's work and ask insightful questions.
5. **Follow Up**: This is where many people drop the ball. If you've had a meaningful interaction, make sure to follow up with a thank-you email or a LinkedIn connection within 48 hours.
6. **Keep Records**: After each networking event, jot down important details about the people you've met, what you discussed, and any follow-up actions. This will be invaluable when you interact with them in the future.
7. **Be Yourself**: Authenticity goes a long way in forming meaningful connections. You're not just selling your skills; you're also showing who you are as a person.
8. **Practice Empathy**: Try to understand the other person's perspective and needs. This will help you offer value in the relationship, making it mutually beneficial.
9. **Regular Check-Ins**: Networking is not a one-off activity. Periodically check in with your contacts to share updates or interesting articles, or simply to ask how they're doing.

Leveraging Social Media

1. **LinkedIn**: This is the go-to platform for professional networking.

- **Profile**: Make sure your profile is complete and up-to-date, including a professional photo and a compelling summary.
- **Connections**: Connect with colleagues, industry leaders, and alumni. Personalize your connection requests with a brief message.
- **Engagement**: Regularly post updates, share articles, and engage

with your network's content. This keeps you on people's radar.

1. **Twitter**: A less formal but equally powerful networking tool.

- **Follow and Engage**: Follow industry leaders, join relevant conversations, and don't hesitate to jump into threads where you can offer value.
- **Tweet Chats**: Participate in industry-specific tweet chats to meet new people and showcase your expertise.

1. **Facebook and Instagram**: While generally more personal, these platforms offer various groups and communities where you can network.

- **Join Groups**: Look for industry-specific groups and participate in discussions.
- **DMs**: If someone's work genuinely interests you, a respectful direct message asking for advice or proposing a collaboration can go a long way.

1. **Personal Blog or Website**: This can serve as an extended resume, showcasing your work, your skills, and your personality.

- **Share Content**: Regularly update your blog with articles, project showcases, or industry insights and share these on your social media platforms.

1. **Networking Apps**: Apps like Shapr or Bumble Bizz are designed specifically for professional networking. They can be particularly useful for introverts or those who find traditional networking overwhelming.

Networking is an ongoing process that requires consistent effort. For women with ADHD, it may require some additional strategies and supports, but the payoff is well worth it. By forming meaningful connections and leveraging the power of social media, you can significantly expand your professional opportunities.

In the next chapter, we'll delve into the topic of long-term career planning, offering advice on how to set and achieve your career goals over the years and decades.

Thank you for joining us in this detailed chapter. With these networking strategies and social media tips, you're well-equipped to expand your professional circle, opening doors to new opportunities and career growth.

V

Mental and Emotional Well-being

12

Stress Management

Stress is an inevitable part of any career, but for women with ADHD, it can be particularly challenging to manage. The symptoms of ADHD, such as impulsivity, distractibility, and difficulty with time management, can exacerbate workplace stress, creating a vicious cycle. In this chapter, we'll delve into coping mechanisms for managing stress effectively and discuss the importance of maintaining a work-life balance.

Coping Mechanisms for Workplace Stress

1. **Identify Stress Triggers**: The first step in managing stress is identifying what triggers it. Is it a particular type of task, a specific colleague, or perhaps the environment you're working in? Knowing the source can help you develop targeted coping strategies.
2. **Time Management**: As discussed in earlier chapters, effective time management can significantly reduce stress. Use tools and techniques like time-blocking, the Pomodoro Technique, or to-do lists to manage your time better.
3. **Mindfulness and Meditation**: These practices have been shown to reduce stress and improve focus. Even a few minutes of deep

breathing or mindfulness meditation can help you reset and reduce stress.
4. **Physical Exercise**: Regular physical activity releases endorphins, which act as natural stress relievers. Even a quick walk during your lunch break can make a difference.
5. **Talk It Out**: Sometimes, discussing your stressors with a trusted colleague, friend, or family member can provide a new perspective and lighten your emotional load.
6. **Professional Help**: If stress becomes unmanageable, consider seeking help from a psychologist or counselor who specializes in stress management or ADHD.
7. **Set Boundaries**: Learn to say no to additional tasks or responsibilities that you can't handle. Overcommitting will only lead to more stress.
8. **Take Breaks**: Short breaks during the workday can help you recharge and reduce stress. Step away from your desk, stretch, or do a quick mindfulness exercise.
9. **Celebrate Small Wins**: The workplace can often be focused on what's going wrong or what needs to improve. Take time to celebrate your achievements, no matter how small, to boost your morale.

Importance of Work-Life Balance

1. **Define Your Priorities**: Work is important, but it's not everything. Make sure you're allocating time to family, hobbies, and other activities that bring you joy and relaxation.
2. **Unplug**: In today's digital age, it's easy to be connected to work 24/7. Make it a point to unplug once you're off the clock. This means no checking work emails or taking work calls during your personal time, unless absolutely necessary.

3. **Flexible Work Arrangements**: If your job allows it, consider flexible work arrangements like remote work or flexible hours to better balance your work and personal life.
4. **Vacation Time**: Use your vacation days. You've earned them, and they're there for a reason. A break from work can help you recharge and reduce stress.
5. **Self-Care**: Allocate time each week for self-care activities that you enjoy and that make you feel relaxed. This could be anything from reading a book to a spa day.
6. **Family and Social Support**: A strong support network can act as a buffer against stress. Spend quality time with loved ones and engage in social activities that make you happy.
7. **Set Realistic Goals**: Ambition is good, but unrealistic expectations can lead to burnout. Set achievable goals for both your work and personal life.
8. **Regular Check-Ins**: Periodically assess your work-life balance. Are you constantly working late? Are you neglecting your personal life? Make adjustments as needed.

Managing stress and maintaining a work-life balance are not just good for your mental health; they're crucial for long-term career success. Overworked, stressed employees are less productive, more prone to errors, and more likely to leave their jobs.

In the next chapter, we'll explore career advancement, focusing on how to climb the corporate ladder while managing the symptoms of ADHD.

Thank you for joining us in this comprehensive chapter. With these stress management techniques and work-life balance strategies, you're well-equipped to handle the pressures of the professional world, ensuring not just career success but also personal well-being.

13

Building Self-Esteem

Self-esteem is the cornerstone of a fulfilling, successful career. For women with ADHD, however, building and maintaining self-esteem can be a complex challenge, often compounded by the stigma associated with ADHD. In this chapter, we'll explore strategies for overcoming this stigma and focus on celebrating your unique strengths.

Overcoming the Stigma of ADHD

1. **Educate Yourself and Others**: The first step in combating stigma is education. Understand what ADHD is and what it isn't. The more you know, the better you can explain it to others, dispelling myths and misconceptions.
2. **Open Dialogue**: If you're comfortable, consider being open about your ADHD diagnosis with trusted colleagues and supervisors. This can help normalize the condition and may even encourage others to share their own experiences.
3. **Seek Support**: Join ADHD support groups, either in-person or online. Sharing your experiences with others who understand can be incredibly validating.
4. **Challenge Negative Thoughts**: Pay attention to your internal

dialogue. If you find yourself thinking, "I'm lazy" or "I'm not good enough," challenge those thoughts. Replace them with more constructive thoughts like, "I'm working on improving my focus" or "I have unique skills that are valuable."

5. **Advocate for Yourself**: As discussed in previous chapters, self-advocacy is crucial. Whether it's requesting workplace accommodations or standing up against discriminatory behavior, advocating for yourself can boost your self-esteem.
6. **Consult a Professional**: If the stigma associated with ADHD is significantly impacting your self-esteem and quality of life, consider consulting a psychologist or counselor who can provide targeted strategies for improvement.

Celebrating Your Unique Strengths

1. **Identify Your Strengths**: Take some time to list your strengths. These could be skills like creativity, problem-solving, or the ability to think outside the box—traits often found in individuals with ADHD.
2. **Leverage Your Strengths**: Once you've identified your strengths, look for ways to leverage them in your job. If you're a creative thinker, for example, volunteer for projects that require creative solutions.
3. **Set Achievable Goals**: Setting and achieving small goals can provide a significant boost to your self-esteem. Make sure your goals are Specific, Measurable, Achievable, Relevant, and Time-bound (SMART).
4. **Celebrate Wins**: Don't wait for a big promotion or a major project completion to celebrate. Small wins, like meeting a challenging deadline or receiving positive feedback, deserve celebration too.
5. **Positive Affirmations**: Create a list of positive affirmations that

resonate with you. Repeat these to yourself, especially when you're feeling low or facing a challenge.
6. **Seek Feedback**: Don't shy away from asking for feedback, both positive and negative. Positive feedback can boost your self-esteem, while constructive criticism can provide valuable insights for improvement.
7. **Maintain a Success Journal**: Keep a journal where you note down your achievements, however small. Review this journal regularly to remind yourself of your capabilities and accomplishments.
8. **Be Kind to Yourself**: Self-compassion is crucial for building self-esteem. Understand that everyone makes mistakes and faces challenges; it's part of being human. What matters is how you learn and grow from them.

Building self-esteem is a continuous journey, one that requires conscious effort and self-reflection. For women with ADHD, this journey may have its unique set of challenges, but it's important to remember that your diagnosis is just a part of who you are, not your entire identity.

In the next chapter, we'll delve into the topic of career transitions, offering advice on how to navigate job changes, whether they are voluntary or imposed.

Thank you for joining us in this comprehensive chapter. With these strategies for overcoming stigma and celebrating your unique strengths, you're well on your way to building a robust sense of self-esteem, empowering you to face the challenges and opportunities of the professional world with confidence.

VI

Career Advancement

14

Climbing the Corporate Ladder

Climbing the corporate ladder is a common career goal, but for women with ADHD, it can seem like a daunting task. The challenges of ADHD, such as impulsivity, distractibility, and time management issues, can make the path to leadership roles seem steep. However, with the right strategies and preparation, you can not only climb the corporate ladder but also excel in leadership positions. In this chapter, we'll explore effective strategies for career advancement and how to prepare for leadership roles.

Strategies for Career Advancement

1. **Skill Development**: Continuously update and expand your skill set. Whether it's taking a course, attending workshops, or simply learning from your daily tasks, skill development is crucial for career advancement.
2. **Networking**: As discussed in previous chapters, networking is invaluable. Build relationships with people who can provide mentorship, offer new opportunities, or simply vouch for your skills and character.

3. **Visibility**: Make sure your efforts and achievements are visible to decision-makers within the organization. This doesn't mean bragging but rather strategically showcasing your work.
4. **Take Initiative**: Volunteer for projects, especially those that are high-visibility or directly aligned with organizational goals. Taking initiative shows leadership potential.
5. **Seek Feedback and Act on It**: Regularly ask for feedback from supervisors, peers, and even subordinates. Use this feedback for continuous improvement.
6. **Be Reliable and Consistent**: Consistency and reliability are traits that managers look for when considering promotions. Make sure you're someone your team can count on.
7. **Negotiate**: Whether it's salary, job responsibilities, or promotions, don't be afraid to negotiate. Know your worth and be prepared to articulate it.
8. **Plan and Set Goals**: Have a clear career path in mind and set achievable, incremental goals towards it. Review and adjust these goals periodically.

How to Prepare for Leadership Roles

1. **Understand Leadership Styles**: Different leadership roles require different styles. Understand what style is most natural for you and how it fits with the leadership role you're aiming for.
2. **Develop Emotional Intelligence**: Leadership isn't just about technical skills; it's also about managing people. Emotional intelligence, the ability to understand and manage your own emotions as well as those of others, is crucial for effective leadership.
3. **Learn to Delegate**: As you move up the ladder, you'll need to delegate tasks. This can be challenging for people with ADHD, who may prefer to have control over every detail. Practice delegation

and trust your team to execute.
4. **Conflict Resolution Skills**: Learn how to manage conflicts effectively. This includes not just resolving disputes but also facilitating a harmonious work environment.
5. **Financial Acumen**: Understand the basics of budgeting, forecasting, and financial reporting, as these are often part of leadership roles.
6. **Communication Skills**: Effective communication is even more critical in leadership positions. Whether it's one-on-one conversations, team meetings, or company-wide presentations, you'll need to communicate clearly and effectively.
7. **Mentorship and Coaching**: Consider seeking a mentor who has experience in leadership roles. Their guidance can be invaluable as you prepare to take on more significant responsibilities.
8. **Self-Care**: Leadership roles come with increased stress and responsibilities. Maintain a healthy work-life balance and stress management techniques to ensure you're up to the task.

Climbing the corporate ladder while managing ADHD is not an easy feat, but it's entirely possible with the right strategies and mindset. By focusing on skill development, networking, and preparing yourself for the challenges of leadership, you can pave the way for a fulfilling and successful career.

15

Entrepreneurship and ADHD

Entrepreneurship is an exciting path that offers the promise of independence, creativity, and potentially, financial freedom. For women with ADHD, entrepreneurship can be particularly appealing as it allows for a level of autonomy and flexibility that traditional employment often lacks. However, it also comes with its own set of challenges that require careful planning and execution. In this chapter, we'll explore tips for starting your own business and look at case studies of successful women entrepreneurs who have ADHD.

Tips for Starting Your Own Business

1. **Business Plan**: The first step in any entrepreneurial venture is creating a comprehensive business plan. This should outline your business idea, target market, competition analysis, financial projections, and marketing strategy.
2. **Legal Structure**: Decide on the legal structure of your business—sole proprietorship, partnership, LLC, or corporation—as each has its own tax implications and filing requirements.
3. **Funding**: Determine your startup costs and how you'll finance

the business. This could be through personal savings, bank loans, or investors.
4. **Market Research**: Understand your target market and customer needs. This will help you refine your product or service and develop an effective marketing strategy.
5. **Product Development**: Whether it's a physical product or a service, focus on creating something that solves a problem or fulfills a need in a unique way.
6. **Branding and Marketing**: Develop a strong brand identity and marketing plan. Utilize social media, SEO, and other digital marketing tools to reach your target audience.
7. **Sales and Distribution**: Decide on how you'll sell your product or service. This could be through an online store, retail partners, or a physical storefront.
8. **Financial Management**: Keep meticulous records of all financial transactions, including expenses and revenue. Consider hiring an accountant or using accounting software.
9. **Time Management**: Use tools and techniques to manage your time effectively, especially since you'll be wearing multiple hats as an entrepreneur.
10. **Adapt and Evolve**: Be prepared to adapt your business model based on customer feedback and market trends. Flexibility can be a significant advantage in the entrepreneurial world.

Case Studies of Successful Women Entrepreneurs with ADHD

1. **Sarah – The Creative Designer**: Sarah was always passionate about fashion but found traditional employment stifling. Her ADHD symptoms made it difficult to adhere to a 9-to-5 schedule. She started her own fashion line, utilizing her creative strengths. Her unique designs quickly gained attention, and she now runs a

successful online store.

2. **Emily – The Tech Innovator**: Emily had a knack for coding but struggled with the rigid structure of corporate life. She started a tech consultancy, leveraging her problem-solving skills to create custom software solutions for businesses. Her firm now employs over 20 people and has clients worldwide.

3. **Rachel – The Food Blogger Turned Restaurateur**: Rachel always had a love for cooking and started a food blog as a hobby. Her unique recipes, coupled with her engaging writing style (thanks to her ADHD-fueled creativity), gained a massive following. She leveraged this success to open her own restaurant, which has received critical acclaim.

4. **Sophia – The Social Impact Entrepreneur**: Sophia was passionate about environmental sustainability. She started a company that produces eco-friendly household products. Her ADHD gave her the drive and energy to navigate the complexities of product development, certification, and marketing. Her products are now sold in stores nationwide.

5. **Lisa – The ADHD Coach**: After years of struggling with ADHD in corporate roles, Lisa decided to become a certified ADHD coach. She used her firsthand experience to help others manage their symptoms and achieve success in their personal and professional lives.

Entrepreneurship offers an exciting avenue for women with ADHD to channel their unique strengths into a fulfilling and potentially lucrative career. However, it's essential to approach it with the same level of planning, research, and execution as you would any other career path.

VII

Special Circumstances

16

Remote Work and ADHD

Remote work has become increasingly prevalent, especially in the wake of global events that have necessitated more flexible work arrangements. For women with ADHD, remote work can be both a blessing and a challenge. The flexibility is often highly beneficial, but the lack of structure can exacerbate ADHD symptoms. In this chapter, we'll delve into how to stay productive while working remotely and tips for setting up an ADHD-friendly home office.

How to Stay Productive While Working Remotely

1. **Create a Routine**: One of the biggest challenges of remote work is the lack of a structured environment. Create a daily routine that mimics a regular workday to help you stay on track.
2. **Time Management Techniques**: Utilize time management methods like the Pomodoro Technique, time-blocking, or the Eisenhower Box to prioritize and manage tasks effectively.
3. **Set Boundaries**: Make it clear to family or housemates that during work hours, you should not be disturbed. This helps maintain a professional environment even when you're at home.

4. **Regular Breaks**: Take short, regular breaks to stretch, walk, or do some quick exercises. This can help improve focus and reduce the monotony of sitting at a desk all day.
5. **Accountability**: Use accountability tools or partners to keep you on track. This could be a co-worker, a friend, or even accountability software that monitors your work.
6. **Communication**: Keep the lines of communication open with your team. Regular check-ins via video calls or instant messaging can help you feel connected and provide opportunities for collaborative work.
7. **Avoid Multitasking**: With the home environment full of distractions, it's tempting to multitask. However, this can be particularly detrimental for individuals with ADHD. Focus on one task at a time for better productivity.
8. **End-of-Day Review**: At the end of each workday, review what you've accomplished and what needs to be tackled the next day. This helps you start each day with a clear plan.

Setting Up an ADHD-Friendly Home Office

1. **Choose the Right Location**: Pick a quiet and comfortable space for your home office. Avoid areas with high foot traffic or external distractions.
2. **Ergonomic Furniture**: Invest in ergonomic furniture like a comfortable chair and a desk at the right height. This can make a significant difference in your ability to focus.
3. **Organized Workspace**: Use organizers, shelves, and drawers to keep your workspace tidy. Clutter can be distracting, especially for someone with ADHD.
4. **Natural Light and Ventilation**: If possible, set up your workspace near a window. Natural light and fresh air can improve mood and

productivity.
5. **Technology Setup**: Ensure you have all the technological tools you need, including a reliable internet connection, necessary software, and any specialized equipment your job may require.
6. **Noise Management**: If noise is a concern, consider noise-cancelling headphones or white noise machines to block out distractions.
7. **Personal Touch**: Add some personal touches like plants, artwork, or motivational quotes to make the space inviting. However, avoid over-decorating as it can become a distraction.
8. **Accessibility**: Keep all frequently used items within arm's reach. This reduces the need to get up frequently, which can break your focus.

Remote work presents a unique set of challenges and opportunities for women with ADHD. By creating a structured routine and an ADHD-friendly home office, you can capitalize on the benefits of remote work while mitigating potential downsides.

Thank you for joining us in this comprehensive chapter. With these strategies for remote work productivity and setting up an ADHD-friendly home office, you're well-equipped to navigate the world of remote work, leveraging its advantages while effectively managing its challenges.

17

Navigating Career Transitions

Career transitions are a natural part of the professional journey, but they can be particularly challenging for women with ADHD. Whether you're considering a career change, re-entering the workforce after a hiatus, or dealing with gaps in employment, this chapter will provide actionable advice to navigate these transitions successfully.

Tips for Changing Careers or Re-Entering the Workforce

1. **Self-Assessment**: Before making any significant career move, take some time to assess your skills, interests, and career goals. This will help you identify the right path for your next chapter.
2. **Research**: Once you have a direction in mind, research the industry, roles, and companies that interest you. This will help you understand the qualifications you'll need and the challenges you might face.
3. **Skill Gap Analysis**: Compare your current skill set with the requirements of your desired role. Identify any gaps and make a plan to acquire the necessary skills, whether through formal education, online courses, or on-the-job training.

4. **Networking**: Utilize your professional network to gain insights into your chosen field. Informational interviews can be particularly helpful in understanding the nuances of a new industry.
5. **Update Resume and LinkedIn**: Tailor your resume and LinkedIn profile to highlight the skills and experiences most relevant to your new career path.
6. **Cover Letter**: Use your cover letter to explain your career transition. Focus on why you're making the change and how your existing skills are transferable to the new role.
7. **Mock Interviews**: Practice interviews with a friend or mentor, focusing on how to present your career transition as a positive move.
8. **Be Prepared for Setbacks**: Career transitions are rarely smooth sailing. Be prepared for setbacks and have a contingency plan in place.

How to Handle Gaps in Employment

1. **Be Honest but Brief**: When explaining employment gaps, honesty is crucial. However, you don't need to go into extensive detail. A brief, straightforward explanation is usually sufficient.
2. **Focus on Productivity**: If your employment gap was spent on personal development, freelancing, or volunteer work, make sure to highlight this. It shows that you were proactive and productive during your time away from full-time employment.
3. **Skill Development**: If you acquired new skills during your employment gap, whether through formal education or self-learning, be sure to mention this in your resume and interviews.
4. **Consult a Career Coach**: If you're struggling to present your employment gap in a positive light, consider consulting a career coach who specializes in career transitions.

5. **Networking**: Use your network to vouch for your skills and work ethic. Personal recommendations can go a long way in overcoming the stigma of an employment gap.
6. **Temporary or Contract Work**: If you're finding it challenging to secure full-time employment, consider temporary or contract positions. These can fill the employment gap on your resume and may lead to permanent roles.
7. **Be Confident**: Confidence is key when explaining employment gaps. If you're comfortable and confident in your explanation, potential employers are more likely to be as well.

Navigating career transitions with ADHD can be a complex endeavor, but with careful planning, self-assessment, and a proactive approach, you can successfully change careers, re-enter the workforce, or handle employment gaps.

Thank you for joining us in this comprehensive chapter. Armed with these tips for career transitions and handling employment gaps, you're well-equipped to navigate the complexities of the professional world, leveraging the unique strengths and overcoming the challenges that come with ADHD.

VIII

Future Outlook

18

ADHD and the Evolving Workplace

The modern workplace is undergoing significant changes, many of which have the potential to impact women with ADHD positively. From technological advancements to shifts in organizational culture, these changes are making workplaces more inclusive and adaptable. In this chapter, we'll explore how the workplace is evolving to be more inclusive and discuss future trends that could benefit women with ADHD.

How the Workplace is Changing to Be More Inclusive

1. **Remote Work**: The rise of remote work has been a game-changer for many people with ADHD who find traditional office environments challenging. Remote work allows for a more personalized work environment, which can be tailored to individual needs.
2. **Flexible Hours**: More companies are offering flexible work hours, allowing employees to work during their peak productivity times. This is particularly beneficial for people with ADHD, who may have varying levels of focus and energy throughout the day.
3. **Diversity and Inclusion Initiatives**: Many organizations are

actively working to create more diverse and inclusive workplaces. This often includes accommodations for neurodiverse individuals, including those with ADHD.
4. **Technology Tools**: The proliferation of productivity and organizational tools can be especially helpful for managing ADHD symptoms. Apps for time management, task tracking, and reminders are more sophisticated and accessible than ever.
5. **Mental Health Support**: There's a growing recognition of the importance of mental health in the workplace. Many companies now offer mental health resources and support, which can include ADHD coaching and therapy.
6. **Skills Over Credentials**: The focus on skills rather than formal qualifications in hiring practices is opening doors for those who may have struggled with traditional educational paths due to ADHD.

Future Trends That Could Benefit Women with ADHD

1. **AI and Automation**: As repetitive tasks become automated, the human workforce will be increasingly focused on creative, problem-solving roles. These are areas where many people with ADHD excel.
2. **Gig Economy**: The rise of freelance and contract work offers more opportunities for project-based roles, which can be ideal for the ADHD work style of intense focus for short periods.
3. **Holistic Employee Well-being**: Future workplaces are likely to take a more holistic approach to employee well-being, including mental health. This could lead to more widespread acceptance and accommodation of neurodiversity.
4. **Virtual Reality (VR) and Augmented Reality (AR)**: These technologies have the potential to revolutionize training and

development programs, making them more interactive and ADHD-friendly.
5. **Personalized Work Environments**: Advances in technology could allow for increasingly personalized work environments that adapt to individual employees' needs, from lighting and noise levels to work schedules.
6. **Transparency and Open Dialogue**: As workplaces become more inclusive, open dialogue about neurodiversity and other forms of diversity is likely to become more common, reducing stigma and empowering individuals to advocate for their needs.
7. **Lifelong Learning**: The increasing pace of change in the business world will require continuous learning and adaptation, which can be well-suited to the ADHD tendency for hyperfocus on areas of interest.

The evolving workplace offers both challenges and opportunities for women with ADHD. By staying informed about these trends and actively participating in the dialogue around workplace inclusivity, you can help shape a professional environment that not only accommodates but celebrates neurodiversity.

Thank you for joining us in this comprehensive chapter. With an understanding of how the workplace is becoming more inclusive and the future trends that could benefit you, you're well-equipped to navigate the evolving professional landscape, leveraging its opportunities while effectively managing its challenges.

19

Lifelong Learning and Development

In today's fast-paced, ever-changing professional landscape, the importance of continuous learning and development cannot be overstated. For women with ADHD, lifelong learning offers a unique set of opportunities and challenges. In this chapter, we'll delve into the significance of continuous learning and provide resources for further development.

Importance of Continuous Learning

1. **Adaptability**: The business world is in a constant state of flux, influenced by technological advancements, market trends, and global events. Continuous learning enables you to adapt to these changes effectively.
2. **Career Advancement**: The more skills and knowledge you acquire, the more valuable you become in the job market. This can lead to promotions, salary increases, and broader career opportunities.
3. **Personal Fulfillment**: Learning new skills or deepening your knowledge in a particular area can be incredibly fulfilling. This

sense of achievement can boost your self-esteem and overall well-being.
4. **Networking**: Educational settings, whether online courses, workshops, or conferences, offer excellent opportunities for networking. You can meet professionals in your field, learn from their experiences, and even find mentors.
5. **Staying Competitive**: As more people enter the job market with advanced skills and qualifications, continuous learning is essential to remain competitive.
6. **Mitigating ADHD Challenges**: Learning new organizational and time-management techniques can help you manage ADHD symptoms more effectively.

Resources for Further Development

1. **Online Courses**: Websites like Coursera, Udemy, and LinkedIn Learning offer a wide range of courses on everything from technical skills to soft skills like communication and leadership.
2. **Workshops and Seminars**: Many industries have regular workshops, seminars, and conferences. These events are excellent opportunities for hands-on learning and networking.
3. **Books and Journals**: Never underestimate the power of a good book. Whether it's industry-specific journals or self-help books on managing ADHD, reading is a valuable resource for continuous learning.
4. **Podcasts and Webinars**: These are convenient learning tools that you can engage with during commutes or downtime. Many experts host podcasts and webinars covering various professional development topics.
5. **Mentorship**: A mentor can provide personalized guidance tailored to your career goals and challenges. Many organizations

offer formal mentorship programs, or you may find a mentor through networking.
6. **ADHD Coaches**: Specialized ADHD coaches can help you develop strategies for managing your symptoms in the workplace, improving your productivity and job satisfaction.
7. **Community Colleges and Adult Education**: Many community colleges offer adult education programs designed for working professionals. These courses can be a cost-effective way to acquire new skills.
8. **Company Training Programs**: Take advantage of any training and development programs offered by your employer. These are often tailored to the skills most relevant to your job.
9. **Social Media Groups**: LinkedIn and other social media platforms have numerous groups dedicated to professional development and industry-specific knowledge.
10. **Self-Directed Learning**: Don't underestimate the value of independent study. The internet offers a wealth of free resources, from tutorials to research papers, that you can use to educate yourself.

Continuous learning is a journey, not a destination. By embracing a mindset of lifelong learning, you not only enhance your professional prospects but also enrich your personal life. For women with ADHD, the dynamic, ever-changing nature of continuous learning can be particularly engaging, offering an outlet for your energy, creativity, and insatiable curiosity.

In the final chapter of this book, we'll summarize the key takeaways and provide a roadmap for your journey ahead in the professional world with ADHD.

Thank you for joining us in this comprehensive chapter. Armed with an understanding of the importance of lifelong learning and a plethora of resources for further development, you're well-equipped to continue growing and adapting in your career, leveraging the unique strengths and overcoming the challenges that come with ADHD.

IX

Conclusion

20

Your ADHD, Your Success

As we conclude this journey, it's essential to reflect on the key takeaways and look forward to the opportunities and challenges that lie ahead. ADHD is a part of you, but it doesn't define you. In this chapter, we'll summarize the essential points from the book and offer some final words of encouragement and advice.

Summary of Key Takeaways

1. **Understanding ADHD**: The first step in navigating the professional world with ADHD is understanding the condition itself—its symptoms, how it manifests differently in women, and common misconceptions.
2. **Diagnosis and Treatment**: A professional diagnosis is crucial for effective management of ADHD. Treatment options can include medication, therapy, and lifestyle changes.
3. **Career Choices**: Selecting a career that aligns with your ADHD traits can set the stage for long-term success. Different job types have their pros and cons, so choose wisely.
4. **Job Interviews and Workplace Accommodations**: Prepare

for interviews in a way that allows you to present your ADHD as a strength. Know your legal rights regarding workplace accommodations and don't hesitate to request them.
5. **Time Management and Organization**: Utilize tools and strategies to manage your time effectively and stay organized, both crucial skills for professional success.
6. **Communication and Self-Advocacy**: Effective communication is key in any job. Learn how to advocate for yourself and build a support network within the workplace.
7. **Networking and Personal Development**: Networking can open doors, and continuous personal development ensures you stay relevant in your field.
8. **Managing Stress and Building Self-Esteem**: Develop coping mechanisms for workplace stress and focus on building your self-esteem to overcome the stigma associated with ADHD.
9. **Career Advancement and Transitions**: Be proactive in seeking career advancement opportunities and prepare adequately for any career transitions, including handling employment gaps.
10. **The Evolving Workplace**: Stay abreast of how workplaces are becoming more inclusive and how future trends could benefit women with ADHD.
11. **Lifelong Learning**: Embrace a mindset of continuous learning to adapt to the ever-changing professional landscape.

Encouragement and Final Words of Advice

1. **Embrace Your Uniqueness**: Your ADHD comes with a unique set of strengths—creativity, problem-solving ability, and often, a different way of looking at the world. Embrace these strengths and use them to your advantage.
2. **Be Your Own Advocate**: No one knows your needs better than

you do. Don't be afraid to speak up and advocate for yourself in the workplace.
3. **Seek Support**: Whether it's friends, family, mentors, or professionals like ADHD coaches and therapists, a strong support network is invaluable.
4. **Never Stop Learning**: The world is full of opportunities for those willing to learn and adapt. Keep an open mind and never stop educating yourself.
5. **Celebrate Small Wins**: The journey may be long and filled with challenges, but don't forget to celebrate the small victories along the way. Each one is a step towards your ultimate goal.
6. **Be Kind to Yourself**: You will have setbacks; that's a part of life, ADHD or not. What matters is how you handle them. Be kind to yourself and use them as learning experiences.
7. **Look Forward, Not Back**: Don't dwell on past mistakes or challenges. Focus on the opportunities that lie ahead and the steps you can take to seize them.

As we close this book, remember that ADHD is a part of you, but it's not the sum total of who you are or what you can achieve. With the right strategies, support, and mindset, you can not only navigate the professional world successfully but also thrive in it.

Thank you for joining us on this journey. Armed with these key takeaways and final words of advice, you're well-equipped to face the professional world, leveraging the unique strengths and overcoming the challenges that come with ADHD. Here's to your success!

www.ingramcontent.com/pod-product-compliance
Lightning Source LLC
Chambersburg PA
CBHW031202020426
42333CB00013B/772